3-31-75

GEMS FROM JAMES

by
Donald Charles Lacy

DORRANCE & COMPANY
Philadelphia

The Scripture quotations in this book are from the
Revised Standard Version Bible and used by permission.

1851211

CONTENTS

PREFACE

With the many "new" ways that are sweeping the churches these days, one gets the idea that a practical, personal, conservative, and evangelistic sermon is just another part of our religious experience that needs to be relegated to the Church's past. As a committed pastor, I am deeply concerned by this. There is much to be commended in the so-called contemporary forms of worship. But let us—in the name of Jesus Christ—not forget our Protestant heritage, which gives primacy to the sermon as God's Word spoken to sinners in need of a Savior and Lord. As attendance at worship and interest in the Church continue to slip in nearly every denomination, surely we can see the message that comes out loud and clear: "novelty for the sake of novelty and change for the sake of change" is a disease making inroads into the authenticity of the Protestant churches across our land.

The Book of James has warmed my heart and excited my mind. This book is a serious study of it, complete with a series of sermons I recommend to every congregation and every pastor. The experience is a magnificent tonic, which is like a "balm in Gilead."

—Donald Charles Lacy

ROUTE OF RUIN

Let no one say when he is tempted, "I am tempted by God"; for God cannot be tempted with evil and he himself tempts no one; but each person is tempted when he is lured and enticed by his own desire. Then desire when it has conceived gives birth to sin; and sin when it is full-grown brings forth death.

—*James 1:13-15*

In the state of Indiana we take a driver's test on traffic signs every four years. The sign that is octagonal or eight sided always means a complete and total "stop." The one that is triangular is the "almost" sign. It means "stop" *if* any car is coming on the intersecting road or street. The round sign always means you are within a few hundred feet of a railroad crossing. The diamond-shaped sign means "warning." The rectangular sign gives various forms of information. Besides all of these, in Indiana there are the unique and not-too-pleasant signs or markers. They are the little crosses we see that designate someone has been killed.

For now, let us concentrate on the warning sign, the stop sign, and the crosses. The latter seems to be about as abundant in some localities as all the other signs combined. Each of these three signs mark the "route of ruin." Each tells us—in plain language with an appropriate designation—where we are on the route. There are opportunities to react favorably to every one of them. As one travels the route, each sign becomes more serious than the previous one. From general observation, it would appear that we pay about as much attention to our spiritual markers as we do to those along our roadways. Some days we pay close attention. Other

1

days we do not bother. Nevertheless, each section of the route of ruin is well marked.

The Letter of James in the New Testament is one of the general or catholic epistles. It is directed to Christians generally. The author speaks like a preaching prophet.

Section one of the route of ruin is marked by the warning signs and is called: *Temptation comes when a person is lured and enticed by his own desire.*

There is an innocent helplessness in our humanity. To be lured and enticed by our own desires is to re-emphasize the old, painful truth of being human. Perhaps this is the most common meeting ground for Christians and non-Christians alike. In the deepest sense, we are all God's children. Confidentially, it may be this meeting ground that keeps you and me Christian. Our spiritual pride can get away from us and cause the Christian witness to be the exact opposite of what it is intended to be. We find that the purification process which every Christian experiences never completely cleans every area of our total existence. Besides being faithful, hopeful, and loving, the disciples of Christ are to be humble and willing to be a part of humanity—a regenerate part, but nonetheless, still a part. Our innocence is a truth. Who can dehumanize himself or herself? Who would like to? If God were to take away our human status, we would no longer be created in His image. I wouldn't like that, would you? Who wants to take out of life the essential kick which enables us to be inspiring saints one day and wretched sinners the next? We are not necessarily speaking of a "split personality." We are simply saying, "Doggone it, I'm just morally helpless in some respects." I am not talking only of sex. It may be easy for some to weigh everything morally in terms of sex. If such is the case, it's too bad, and maybe pathetic. One may never have committed adultery; but one may have been guilty of just about everything else, including a blasphemous spirit toward God.

There has to be an honest confrontation. The diamond sign marked "warning" is there. The fact of our temptation is

2

there. A rose by any other name is still a rose. Temptation by any other name is still temptation. It is no sin to be human, but to be human is to be capable of sin. Who among us can say he or she is not tempted? What are your feelings? What are your thoughts? Do you feel like having an affair with a married man? Are you thinking of bearing false witness by putting someone you dislike into a very negative light that may jeopardize his whole future? Honesty is always the best policy, and it applies even more therapeutically to our temptations than to the business world. Granted, some honesty is best left unverbalized.

We begin the journey down the route of ruin when we are tempted, lured, and enticed by our own desire. This first part of the route—temptation—you and I must travel. An option is not available. The second part is different. By our own free will, we choose to continue.

Section two of the route is marked by the stop signs and is called: *From temptation to sin.*

Our innocence slips into the background and we admit that we can help ourselves. By now, we are past the warning stage and have entered a stretch of superhighway with stop signs. Must anyone sin? To be sure, we are all converted or unconverted sinners or in the process of becoming one or the other. Yet, who has to sin? At this point, we might lose ourselves in trying to define "sin." Some people do this. In place of really wanting to know more about their spiritual situation, they will evade it by defining, redefining, debating, and discussing. Humans have become exceedingly skillful at this recently. But we only succeed in piling guilt on top of guilt. When you drive up to an intersection with a stop sign, what is the reasonable thing to do? Come to a complete halt, of course. This is also true morally. Once we have come to a complete stop, we can get off the route or, at least, go back to the warning signs. The third chapter, twenty-second verse of Genesis reads: "Then the Lord God said, 'Behold, the man has become like one of us, knowing good and evil. . . . ' " If we

3

do not heed the eight-sided sign when driving, most anything can happen to us; this is also true in the moral and religious sense.

As we roar or even just roll past the moral stop sign, remember what our Lord said to a woman centuries ago: He told her to sin no more. He didn't say she would never be tempted again. I think each of us recognizes the relativity of all of this, because of the very personal nature of the route of ruin. Another way of putting it is to say each person is intimately responsible.

From the vantage point of situational ethics, as I understand the concept, there are no permanent stop signs. Everything is marked "go—go—go." If we become too critical of this point of view, we can be overly unfair. This ethical approach, at least, has saved some of our young adults from the aimless rigidity and fruitless legalism which held some of their parents and grandparents in spiritual bondage. Let us be sure, however, that we do not allow the moral, unifying cords that hold us together as a people and help individuals from orgiastic abandonment slip from us.

So the second part of the route is the progression from temptation to sin. The stop signs are there. God gave a mind and a will to you and me. We are expected to use that mind rightly and exercise that will properly. Mark Twain once said, in effect, "It isn't what I don't understand about the Bible that bothers me; it is what I do understand." Likewise, it is not the stop signs we don't see that bother us; it is the ones we do see.

There is a final section. It is marked by crosses and is called: *From sin to death.*

Tragedy has arrived, and we are far, far down the road. The warning signs have been ignored. The stop signs have been driven through. Now one's sinning has become commonplace. An adjustment has been made, and life would not be the same without them. The crosses signify not merely physical death, which all of us must experience, but spiritual death. One's eternal destiny is at stake. At any minute one will be called upon by the Creator to account for a soul which has been wasting away. The mortician is prepared to handle the body, and the hearse is ready and waiting. I wish it weren't this way, don't you? Who can say how long this stretch of the route will be? Who can designate those already on it? Spiritual death is extremely personal. There are those who yearn to see just one warning sign.

Immediate repentance followed by a firm resolution to live a changed life is the only answer I know. Perhaps you know a better one. I must confess, this is the only one which comes to me. Repentance is always serious business. At this point on the route of ruin, it is decisive. To live a changed life is an essential product of true repentance. Thank God, there are some walking illustrations! Praise God, during a time when the very heart of the faith is being called into question, the faith still stands any and all tests! If you're on this final part of the route and traveling at such a high rate of speed that the crosses are rushing by, won't you at least slow down long enough to consider that you are on a dead-end roadway? Only you and your God need to know. He has placed the crosses there, hoping you might have a heart-to-heart talk with Him. "It is no secret what God can do, with arms wide open He'll pardon you" is infinitely more than sentimental religion.

At what point are you and I in our many encounters with life? That is, where are you and I on the route of ruin? It is possible to become too introspective and to analyze morbidly oneself all the time. We all know those who do this. What about those who evade themselves by refusing a careful, inward look? God does not expect us to keep track of every minute detail that happens in our lives. With loving simplicity and unimpeachable charity He says, "Come now, my child, be honest with yourself."

Let us not make the route of ruin more complicated than it is. The signs are there. Whether or not we are sure which sign is ahead of us, we should always drive carefully. The good driver is neither the slowest nor the most meticulous. He is careful and exercises much common sense. Although ignoring the signs is a grave offense, the careful driver knows God does not have to catch him. God already knows where he is on the route, and deep down, so does he.

DON'T GET MAD ABOUT IT!

*Know this, my beloved brethren. Let every man be quick
to hear, slow to speak, slow to anger, for the anger of man
does not work the righteousness of God.*

—James 1:19-20

"Don't get mad about it!" is good advice. We are taught
that "mad" technically means "mentally ill, insane, or crazy."
Of course, you and I generally use the word to mean "foolish,
rash, senseless, and unwise." The two understandings are not
as far apart in meaning as some would like to believe. We tend
to be sympathetic on the one plane, while labeling the other
plane childish and infantile. The phenomenon of anger best
reflects both. It is foolishness and a form of spiritual insanity.
It is more than blowing off steam. It is more than just
releasing the inner pressures which make us overly tense.
Anger is accompanied by vindictiveness, chronic petulence,
and even hatred.

"The anger of man does not work the righteousness of
God" is a straightforward religious truth. Our Lord places
grave seriousness on the condition. In Matthew 5:21-22, He
says, "You have heard it was said to the man of old, 'You shall
not kill; and whoever kills shall be liable to judgement.' But I
say to you that every one who is angry with his brother shall be
liable to judgement." This is not to be confused with "righteous anger," which is exemplifed by our Lord driving the
money changers out of the temple. You and I may be outraged
and call it righteous anger, but we learn a few weeks later that
someone simply belittled an idea which we thought was of
supreme importance at the time. It is possible to be angry for

7

righteous reasons, but we have a tendency to overplay this experience.

James provides us with three practical suggestions. He says, "Be quick to hear." We say that there are so many things to hear these days, and we are right. If we follow this advice with all the communications media coming at us and discussions with our friends in between times, we could very easily crack up. We say that James was speaking to a simple world, compared to ours, and we are right again. Nevertheless, it is a worthy suggestion. He says, "Be slow to speak." You and I say that if we do that all the time, we will get run over, and we are at least partially right. How slow is slow? The philosopher of the latter half of our century is apt to reply that it depends on the existential moment, and that appears to be a good answer. At any rate, James's suggestion is still a fine one. He says, "Be slow to anger." From time to time, all of us are like lighted fuses, but I am sure he is speaking of something of far greater importance and more depth. Note, he does not say, "Don't ever get angry." He leaves the door open to the possibility of being "righteously angered." So his third guideline is, likewise, significantly beneficial.

Having said these things, there are a couple of questions to be asked. How do we prevent ourselves from becoming angry—"Don't get mad about it"—and hindering the working of God's righteousness?

Don't we already have answers to these questions? We do. However, we must take them close and meditate upon them.

Be quick to hear.

What meaning do we discover? Well, in our world we are instantaneously confronted with a scale of priorities. Whom should we hear? Fifty years ago or less this was not much of a problem. Long working hours, poor transportation, and a lack of communication severely limited human contact. Now, and for the past several years, we must decide to whom we will listen. There are always those we must hear, but these people are relatively few. Those who should be heard for their own betterment often are reluctant to speak at any length. Separating whom should be heard from others requires the guidance of the Holy Spirit. Those who need a listening ear must not be met by a pretending professional or amateur. A revealing story is told of a widely-known judge. He passed into the hereafter and met Saint Peter at the pearly gates. Surprisingly, his entrance was delayed. Saint Peter complimented him for his outstanding record, but then said, "You persistently pretend to hear those who were in deep trouble, and, in fact, you never actually heard any of them." The judge was deflated and inquired, "But surely that cannot keep me out of heaven?" Saint Peter replied, "I am afraid it already has."

You and I are required by Christian responsibility to personalize James's first suggestion. Wherever we work, live, play, and worship, let us "be quick to hear." One fellow at the factory is obviously obnoxious, but someone *really* needs to listen to him. The woman two doors away has terrible fits of temper, sending terror into territories far and near, but someone *really* needs to listen to her. This teenage lad at the bowling alley is all tied up in dozens of different knots, but someone *really* needs to listen to him. The lady in the church who has recently retired from her job has problems that are not new to others, but someone *really* needs to listen to her. This day there are particular persons you and I need to hear. Not everyone can or ought to be a counselor in the professional sense of the word. However, aren't Christians and churchmembers, who ought to "be quick to hear," under the leadership of the Holy Spirit?

James's practical point is well taken. His next one is just as valid and must be seen in relation to the first. It may be even more trying than the one initially mentioned.

Be slow to speak.

What do we find in these words? We all like to talk, and some are veritable verbal gushers. Some do so from abundant nervous energy. Some admit they like to hear the sound of their voices. Some believe their proposals are essential to the well-being of themselves and others. Regardless of the motivation, it is nearly always best to hold onto the words and await the proper time for them to be said. Proper timing is more important than quality or quantity of words. The Holy Spirit can and does teach us this. We are reminded that words, once they are spoken, cannot be retrieved. We can write one-hundred letters and tear up all one-hundred letters without anyone, except Almighty God, knowing. Sometimes this is what we should do.

After the battle at Gettysburg, Robert E. Lee's army slipped across the Potomac River into Virginia. The Union general, Meade, seemed to be guilty of an extremely serious military error. President Lincoln was greatly upset. In his anger, Abe wrote a letter to the Union commander. It was harsh and biting. In the quietude of his own personal sanctuary, the President decided not to send it. The outpouring of his bitter feelings, conveyed to the general in a letter, would have only caused much more harm. Even a great man like Lincoln, with dictatorial powers during wartime, could have made a costly mistake by sending the letter to a subordinate. A good letter may be one that is never sent.

If we aren't careful, even well-intended words can cause us to direct the import of the matter into an impersonal file; so, let's not pull that boner. The Word of God reminds us to "be slow to speak" in those relationships which directly touch us. Lest we tend to begin believing "silence is always golden," remember James says nothing of not speaking at all. Ponder for a moment yesterday's human relationships. Were you slow to speak? Think of today. Are you slow to speak? Project yourself into tomorrow and visualize those people who will touch your life. Are you going to be slow to speak? Our religion can stay in the clouds of shallow idealism to the detriment of victorious living in a world with more than a small amount of grime. The firing line is that daily walk you take among fellow human beings.

James describes the way to deal with anger as it appears on the distant horizon. In his trio of practical pointers, he has one more thing to say:

Be slow to anger.

How shall we understand this spiritual command? Christian churchmembers are to have high boiling points. As we grow in the religious life, this temperature moves a little higher. We should not confuse this ideal with brief and sporadic emotional outbursts. Some days we do not feel good. Basically, James is not dealing with this. Anger involves the depths of one's sinfulness. This is why our Lord speaks of it as He does. The angry man is a thoroughly dangerous human being who may inflict pain upon many people. The person controlled by this devil can literally jeopardize the spiritual welfare of multitudes. Is it any wonder we are told to "be slow to anger"? It is possible to follow James's suggestion not by curtailing our human relationships, but by individual discipline and the dictates of the Holy Spirit. Of course, anger is also self-destructive.

Several sailors are marooned on a tropical island. They notice coconuts high in the trees. The coconuts can quench their thirst and ease their hunger. The precious fruit is too high up to be reached. However, there are some chattering monkeys in the trees. The sailors begin to throw stones, sticks, and whatever is handy at them. Eventually, the monkeys are enraged by the intrusion and throw the coconuts down at the sailors. This is exactly what the men wanted. We are not monkeys, but upon occasion, we must admit we are monkeylike.

The anger of a mob is a sight to behold, but one person has to be angry before the mob can come into being. We arrive again at the crux of the matter: personal responsibility. "I am going to take care of myself, because no one else will" is more than a well-worn sentence. It can be applied to you and me at this very instant. You and I are prone to allow others to determine our reactions. Who can make you and me angry,

11

unless we permit them? Why be tempest-tossed and made vicious by forces from outside ourselves? Willpower seems to provoke little respect these days, but each of us is responsible. There are evident exceptions to what is being said, but how many actual illustrations can we definitely cite? A little boy once said about his religious experience, "Oh, there's just me and Jesus." His presence is the saving factor in keeping our daily routine from becoming one of shoving and being shoved.

This is the final of three short charges. In conclusion, we are going to deal with a frank and direct statement from the text, which acts as both a beginning and ending.

"The anger of man does not work the righteousness of God." These words are the reason for the three points of the sermon. The three points are the reason for these words. However we look at it, we still must return to the spiritual truth: Our anger will not work God's righteousness. "Stay out of the way!" is something we can hear at any shipyard on any day of the week. No one has a right to hinder the movement of valuable cargo. The same is true in the operation of God's righteousness. It is better to do nothing than to get mad and stay mad about it. Of course, James has put up some signposts. We are not left without expert advice.

More specifically, where does this leave you and me? The answer is: mainly where we have been in the past, *unless* we vow to do better.

RELIGION WITHOUT BLEMISH

Religion that is pure and undefiled before God and the Father is this: to visit orphans and widows in their affliction, and to keep oneself unstained from the world.

—James 1:27

"Immaculate" is one of those very special words in the English language. It means "totally clean" or "completely pure." We reserve it for those high moments in our lives. Great compliments are paid by saying it—"Her appearance is immaculate"; "His grooming is immaculate." We are not prone to use it loosely, as we do with so many other descriptive words. When someone does, we readily recognize it. We reserve it for special occasions. When it is spoken, we perk up our ears and listen. It is one of the few aristocrats among the hundreds of thousands of words in our language. Some will vie against others just to have the word applied to themselves. The uneducated may not be able to pronounce it. They may not be able to spell it. But they know its value. You and I appreciate its worth. "To be without blemish" is something!

"What is a blemish to one, is not a blemish to another" is good, acceptable reasoning for our own day. We are reminded of the farmer who tries to give an absolute definition for a weed. Soon his wisdom tells him that it can be anything that grows, if it's in the wrong place at the wrong time—a stock of corn in a soy bean field, wheat in a corn field, potatoes in a tomato field, even a rose in a strawberry patch.

Toleration of diverse points of view is an inspiration to us. So much in life is dependent on who we are, where we are, and what time it is. Our enlightenment has created possibilities for growth and development in human relations which far exceed anything our ancestors knew. Even in matters considered strictly religious, this is still the case. This is neither empty activism nor sinning against God's absolute laws. That's just the way we find things in our day.

We can quickly perceive ideas and ideals in James's lesson which have proven their value. Pure and undefiled religion is both "reaching out" and "keeping out." The Christian pulls the world unto himself and bleeds with and for others. The Christian pushes the world away and keeps himself free from sin. There are two dimensions, but one without the other is null and void. We must understand that the two are parts of the same imperative. James means this in a very personal way. Each precious human being who professes the Christian faith is called to go out into the world in the spirit of brotherly service. Each precious human being who professes the Christian faith is called to stay away from the world and be distinctively "without blemish." Our course is clear.

"To visit orphans and widows in their affliction" is *reaching out.*

We are to move out into the world. Our Lord grew up under the influence of a very wise Jewish heritage. Orphans and widows were especially protected by law. They were a symbol of Jewish compassion. Women whose husbands were dead and children who had lost one or both parents were given care. Our Lord's ancestors treated them better than any other nation of people. Our Lord reaffirmed this position. In our day, the passage speaks to us, because we see in the widows and orphans the image of all needy people. The needy are those who, for the most part, will not come to us. We must go to them. As James says, we are "to visit." The Christian visitor may be a man of the cloth or a layman who takes his religion seriously. To "stay at home" may mean several different things. It is certain that it does not mean the needy of the world are continually to seek the help of professing Christians. We are to go to them. Laymen, generally, are not nearly aggressive enough. In the best sense of the word, Christian aggressiveness simply means bold and energetic pursuit in the cause of Christ.

In our day, this can be and is a dynamic way of life. The live-wire life insurance and automobile salesmen are not the only practitioners of "beating the bushes." Every Christian churchmember should be beating the bushes for Christ and His Church. I did not use the phrase "institutional recruitment." Sometimes we communicate the idea that we are only interested in someone's name being on the church rolls. This is important, and don't ever underestimate it. Joining a service club or a sorority is not the same as uniting with the Church of Jesus Christ. There are those who like to draw similarities, and some are legitimate. I am sure the spirit of our Lord and Savior works through such organizations. However, I doubt that Saint Peter will be interested in the size and ornamentation of our organization's pins. There is no more exciting and vital activity than the Christian working in the community in the name of Jesus Christ.

How well do you and I measure up? A common reaction is, "Well, I just naturally reach out in helping those in need." There are dedicated people who, in fact, do this very thing. How many do you know? For those of us who rate a more average standing in the Christian life, it takes some planned or systematic work. When we think the job of going to the spiritually and materially needy is going to be done by those who will naturally do it, we are pulling the wool over our own eyes. The word "Methodist" comes from the word "methodical." John and Charles Wesley practiced methodical study and worship. Our Wesleyan heritage is a great and meaningful one. "Plan your Christian work and work your Christian plan" is a timely message for modern followers in the tradition of the Wesleys. God spoke through the founders of Methodism, and He wants to speak through us.

It is what God considers important that matters. An immaculate religion or one without blemish is on God's terms. The religious experiences of men, women, and youth have been bogged down innumerable times by human beings getting in the way. Through the letter of James come the inspired words that religion which is pure and undefiled before God is "to visit orphans and widows in their affliction. . . ." Broadly speaking, God says, "Go to those in need and minister to them." In our day, because of complicated living, we seem to hang out a shingle here and there which reads: "Professional Christian Problem Solver—Help By Appointment at the Office Only." It is true that the clergy and laity, regardless of their time and talents, have just so much time they can give. It is also true that some will waste our precious time, even under the pretense of needing religious help. Yet, this must never become an alibi which freezes out the reluctant. If the men and women of the church want to serve the needy they say they are concerned about, they must do some visiting—and I don't mean over the telephone. God says a necessary part of religion without blemish is to visit the needy. The church must be taken from the confines of a sanctuary and put in direct contact with those in need.

We have dealt with the first part of the imperative. The second part is no less important. It may appear more or less difficult, depending on our personalities.

"To keep oneself unstained from the world" is *keeping out*.

We are to be separate and apart from secular life and interests. A radical interpretation can cause a serious rupture in our understanding of the faith. On the other hand, let us not explain away the message. Religion without blemish necessarily involves a conservative approach, in terms of our activities. The Christian is deeply and sincerely concerned about everything that goes on in the world, on the moon, and elsewhere. Direct involvement in many questionable areas is not apt to keep one unstained. This is not "the ostrich with his head in the sand" attitude. It is a reaffirmation of the truth the Apostles knew only too well: Christians are different from others; and even though they do not run from worldly affairs, nevertheless, they do stay clear of some surroundings. The early Christians had to face the fact that emperor worship was expected of them. They evaded situations where it had to be practiced. Premeditated martyrdom was not and is not essential in proving one's faith.

Where many present-day Christians get themselves into trouble is by fulfilling only this part of the condition for an immaculate religion. Only sticking one's head out of the house just long enough to gain a livelihood and attend church regularly is disastrous and, in truth, shows "no guts," in modern terminology. Yet, to go on a binge of poking one's Christian nose into every area of the secular world is also a disastrous approach to life. Perhaps the hardest lesson Woodrow Wilson, a Christian president, had to learn was that the world was wicked when he came into it, and it would be wicked when he left it. This kind of realism is not easy for some to come by.

From another point of view, it is difficult but realistically possible to be possessed by a religion which is pure and undefiled. Some preaching may be so idealistic and theoretical that it becomes a theological labyrinth of little or no value, except for intellectual gymnasts. The Letter of James, specifically our present excerpt, never makes that mistake. The words deal with attainable ideals, provable theories, and practical theology. If what James is talking about is "way out there some place," we have drifted too far from the roots of our faith. The first century and New Testament Churches are our spiritual forebears, and we are irrevocably tied to them. There is a gospel song which goes: "It is real, it is real; Thank God the doubts are settled, I know it is real."

How well are you and I doing? The dividing line between Christian concern and "crass nibbiness" is sometimes clouded. It is a line each sensitive Christian has to draw for himself or herself. You and I are under pressure today to "get involved" in anything that has some semblance of salvation. Those of us who have committed ourselves unreservedly to Jesus Christ and His Church *do* hear a very personal voice calling us to be unblemished by pushing away those elements of the world that promise only to hinder.

Again, it is what is important to God that matters. He speaks through His servants. The writers of the New Testament were His servants. God says an essential part of religion without blemish is to keep oneself unsoiled by worldly matters not conducive to the strengthening of the faith. Each of us wrestles with this in the inmost recesses of his or her soul. No preacher or priest can draw up exact specifications for you. This is between you and your God.

Shakespeare wrote, "Above all, to thine own self be true." Religion without blemish says to the Christian, "Above everything else, be true to your best self." When you and I are hard pressed by the vicissitudes of life, we are called upon to be faithful. Perhaps we cannot stand without wavering, but we can hold our ground. Be alert to the needs of the world and do something about them. Be not drowned by the strident voices and cleverly disguised undercurrents of an evil world—a world which will be evil when you and I leave it. By apostolic decree and personal integrity, let us "reach out," but also "keep out."

Holiness before God is all that really matters. It is of supreme importance to be spiritually successful within His boundaries. "To visit orphans and widows in their affliction, and to keep oneself unstained from the world" is sound doctrine. The practical fulfillment of it is holiness before God and wholeness of the individual Christian.

THE MARKS OF A DEAD FAITH

So faith by itself, if it has no works, is dead.
                                              —James 2:17

What is the most depressing sight you have ever seen? Recall some unpleasant memories: pictures of starving children with their swollen stomachs in Africa—an automobile hit by a train, with parts of bodies strewn down the tracks—a parent beating a child for no reason, except to release guilt feelings—an old lady lying in a gutter and bleeding profusely, because she has just been mugged—a soldier in agony on the battlefield, all alone—a pretty young co-ed viciously raped and then mutilated—the character assassination of a man who could not get along in the system—pictures of Hitler's death houses, where millions of Jews were not treated as well as beasts of the field—the suicide of one who seemed to have everything to live for—gross dishonesty by one who has had the trust of many.

Spiritually speaking, a dead faith tops the list. So much of what has previously been mentioned is a simple reflection of the sins and mistakes of our world. A faith which is dead places the finger of judgment on the Church. It implies that there once was a spark. Faith is not supposed to be dead. The two words seem very incompatible and in direct contradiction. This is why they point to a depressing condition. To say "so-and-so is an inactive churchmember" does not convey the true state of affairs. We have to define "inactive." Observing those possessed by a dead faith enables us to see the gravity of the situation. We know the church was not intended to be hamstrung by those whose faith is dead. So we come face to face with what is offensive to God, depressing to those who care, and, in fact, a dastardly sin.

The Letter of James provides a terse, practical, and personal message to Mr., Mrs., or Miss Churchmember: If your faith is one without works, it is lying on the mortician's slab. Those in the first century were already having problems of isolating faith from works. This verse in James attempts to apply the corrective. In letter and spirit it does that very thing.

Our own Protestant heritage is being seriously perverted. To speak in terms of "excess baggage on the membership rolls" is trite and only a cause for being tuned out by those in the suitcases. We are dealing with a far more serious and eternally consequential matter. The centuries have shown us to be people who practiced faith. We have known that works without faith is an odious sin. We must relearn at both the intellectual and emotional levels that faith alone is a sin that points directly to hypocrisy and spiritual death.

A distinction has to be made between the observer and the judge. We are all familiar with the scriptural injunction "Judge not." You and I have neither the right nor the power to bless some into heaven, damn others to hell, or proclaim total extinction for others. We are called upon to be faithful to the faith of our Lord and Savior, and that means saying something about the observable characteristics of a dead faith.

In the first place, there is *the absence of private and public prayer.*

By their own admission, many on the church rolls do not pray privately. They do not go into their secret sanctuaries for serious deliberations with their God. Deep down, you and I know there has never been a vital faith divorced from those hidden in prayer. Is there fear one may really come face to face with one's spiritual poverty? It is interesting how many good things we do not do out of sheer fear. Often, we are clearly and tearfully afraid of what we may see. It is a fact that most people in the United States are living entirely too fast, in terms of not coming to grips with the significance of life as

20

God intended it. What better documentation is there than to hear someone admit that it has been weeks since he secretly consulted with his God. Generally, the minister cannot tell whether or not you have been having private sessions with your Creator. He can only listen with compassion to you, as you own up to such negligent omissions.

Members certainly do not have to be in church to pray publicly, but how many other times and places are conducive? Unless a minister at a banquet asks all to repeat the Lord's Prayer, he intones words for those present. Who among the laity can lead others in prayer? You and I both know what the answer is—almost no one. Yet, we reside in a nation where approximately 60 percent of the population belongs to the Church. For many, Christianity is actually a very dead faith. Some of us become weary of creating opportunities for our people to pray before and with others. Of course, it is natural to want to be entertained, rather than joining in some printed prayer with brothers and sisters in the Body of Christ. If you cannot pray publicly, you can learn to do so—that is, if we serve the arisen Christ we say we serve.

Enough about the initial mark of a dead faith. It is not very difficult to spot. It is quite difficult to remedy without a crisis situation.

In the second place, there is *the refusal to worship in the House of God.*

"Refusal" is the precise word. We have all heard "enlightened discussions" centered around "being right with God and going to church." Do you know a dedicated and inspiring Christian churchmember who does not worship faithfully in his church whenever possible, except for those who are disabled? Do you know an able-bodied person who cannot be present for worship, at least most of the time? In some cases a change in time or the addition of a service will help. In other cases it is only a second chance to say no. Even though we are easy on one another and say we can't make it Sunday, we know there is a "mind set" which has already said, "I am not

21

going." Generally, the churches are not overflowing because a high percentage of the membership consciously or subconsciously has said, "We are not going this morning." If those now reading this book can get one other member to look into the mirror next Saturday evening long enough to confront the issue at hand, your reading is more than for the purpose of evangelistic instruction. You will become an ambassador for stamping out a dead faith, the biggest disease in every church across America.

"Tell it like it is" has become a popular phrase. If we are to follow this suggestion, we might just as well say, "Most of our churchmembers refuse to come to the worship services most of the time." Generally, people have, at least, fifty adult years. That means twenty-six hundred Sundays. If the present trends continue in our churches, many members will have approximately two thousand refusals. I don't know about you, but I would not want to face my God with that kind of record.

A common reaction to a straightforward approach which scalds a bit is, "Why doesn't the pastor talk to those who need it?" Every sensible, busy pastor counts on his members to talk to themselves and to others who need it. Churches have a habit of outlasting pastors. Of course, it may be most churches like it the way it has been. In divine truth, members may repent their sins of omission when the Grim Reaper pays a visit, but his swath will not be any less devastating for the here and now. A carpenter can drive nail after nail into a fine board. If he pulls them out, the repelling holes remain.

Let's call a halt to our discussion about the second mark of a dead faith. If one is honest, it is not very difficult to spot. Like most other adventures in the Christian life, therapy begins with repentance.

In the third place, there is *the disregard of tithing as spiritually essential*.

Have you ever known a dedicated member who did not give at least 10 percent of his or her income to the church and charitable organizations? Let's admit that there is a problem in applying the percentage. Some people figure things differently than others. When a minister hands the offering plates to the ushers, he is sometimes tempted to say, "Let us give freely and generously, in accordance with what we reported on our income tax." Recently, I saw a cartoon with two Roman Catholic priests at work in their spacious study. The younger priest, who was the assistant, was preaching that Sunday. He looked over at the Senior Father and said: "My sermon deals with those who are unwilling to tithe. What's the theological equivalent for 'stinker'?" One lovely church lady who wanted to say something nice to the pastor really didn't prepare much in advance when she said, "Reverend, since we began tithing, we are so contented and peaceful. My dear husband is a genius at figuring deductions and exemptions. We'll actually be giving less this year than before." Tithing is serious business, and it is a spiritual imperative. To regard it on any lesser plane is the mark of a dead faith. But let's not take comfort in how much we think we give to charitable organizations.

There is a concern about this matter which is causing many pastors and leading lay people to do some earnest questioning. When there are two, three, or more incomes in a family, why should only one of them receive the application of the tithe? If the husband is making eight thousand dollars and the family gift is eight hundred dollars, this sounds very exemplary—until we learn the wife is making six thousand dollars and the teenage sons another one thousand dollars. It's all God's money, and all of it is to be tithed. Anything less is a mark of dead faith.

So much for our third point. Some of our lay people have done sober and solemn thinking about their giving. Praise God, there are always those who are willing to grow, even when their worst selves say no. To the continuing detriment of Christ and His Church, most members have never really tried to tithe over a full year.

In the fourth and final place, there is *the failure to serve by giving time.*

"Preacher, what do you mean 'giving time'?" That is a

legitimate question and deserves an answer. There are literally dozens of jobs needing to be done for the church. Some require training, but others do not. Many things in the church would never be done, except for volunteer help. When a person unites with the church, it is reasonably assumed he or she will work the needs of the church. Frequently, the best possible solution for a church of above average size is to assign those tasks which require very little or no prior training. No lay person or pastor likes to be abused in this area, but neither does the church deserve to be refused. Churchmanship is a matter of Christian maturity. Whatever is necessary to get the work load of the church spread among more and more people is usually a good method.

Cooperation is the old-new word which never seems to be overused. For the church to be administered fairly and effectively, the laity *must* be willing to take the responsibility of giving time. The grown-up lay person may not be able to keep an appointment or assignment, but he or she will see to it the work of the church does not suffer, by finding an adequate substitute. Except for a handful of people, the requests of the church for time from the laity are staggeringly small.

This is the fourth mark of a dead faith. For some weary lay people and pastors, it is the easiest to spot. For a fact, many churchmembers are not giving their own church the time of day.

God has given us a will and, as judge, He will decide how well we have utilized it. It is true, in the words of the Apostle, Paul, that "salvation is the gift of God." It is just as true that "churchmanship requires a determined mind which unalterably says, 'The gates of hell cannot prevent me from upholding my church.'" Every individual who belongs to a church has the potential for that kind of churchmanship. A dead faith is something that can be changed.

TEACHING AND POWER

Let not many of you become teachers, my brethren, for you know that we who teach shall be judged with greater strictness.

—*James 3:1*

Teddy Roosevelt said, "A tramp will steal from a railroad car. But if you send him to college and educate him, he will steal the railroad." The power of the teacher and his teachings is illustrated time and again. That power lends itself to both tremendous good and horrendous evil. Those who sit in the chairs of authority in the classroom or any teaching situation are men and women of great influence. How many of the momentous events of our time can be traced directly to a teacher or teachers? The cliche "She who rocks the cradle rules the world" points up the awesome potential power every mother has as a teacher. You and I can line up the pros and cons of teaching materials and methods. We can even debate the attitudes and attributes of particular teachers. Everyone of us quickly owns up to the power involved. So much of what we are, we did not form. This is not fatalistic or intended to relieve us of our responsibility. It is just to say, "Whether it be a private school, a public school, or a Sunday school, we have been and are being molded by teachers." Our Blessed Lord was a teacher. He says in the Gospel of John: "You call me teacher and Lord; and you are right, for so I am."

What do we remember about our teachers? Is it the teaching methods? Is it the teaching materials? No, it's the personality of a human being in a position of authority, isn't it? It seems to me, we are to a large extent what and who we are because of what and who our teachers were and are. Just as teachers teach human students, so do teachers teach by being human beings. What do we remember about Mrs. Jones, back in the fourth grade? Well, let's see—she whipped Tommy, because he refused to spit out his gum; she choked one day on a piece of Christmas candy; and she wrote the names of people she most admired on the blackboard. Oh, yes, we can call to mind some teaching skill, but don't we largely remember her as a person? What do we remember about Mr. Smith, the high school history teacher? Well, let's see—he wore the loudest ties, quivered at the mouth when he became mad, and thought Napoleon Bonaparte was terribly neurotic. We do remember other things of a more educational nature, but his personality is what sticks in our minds. This is generally the story, isn't it? Some say they are being taught by the objectivity of television today, but don't we recall a great deal about Walter Cronkite and others? Even those tied to the microscope and test tubes are entertained by old professor Brown's jokes about the modern birds and bees.

The Letter of James reads: "Let not many of you become teachers, my brethren, for you know that we who teach shall be judged with greater strictness." This verse spiritually rings with the very thing mentioned: the teacher, his teaching, and the power created. How can we better describe this unusual power? Let us hang our ideas upon four words that rhyme: competence, repentance, impotence, and omnipotence.

The teacher and his teachings can give us *competence*.

In our day, social accommodation is of grave consequence. We have to know how to get along with other people. This was an option in the case of our grandfathers and grandmothers. With us, it is a necessity for congenial survival. Most people come into contact with others practically every day they live, and they find it a trying experience to relate well to at least a few of them. The old, new, and potential grudges are there. Sores can be rubbed raw by too much interaction. Those who profess the name of Christ are no different than many others sometimes, because we allow our religion to get in the way by feeling just a little superior. How many times have we heard the excellence of someone's training extolled and then heard the closing words, "but he can't get along with people"? It is unlikely that even the wisest teacher can make us popular. He can give us the tools and insight to get along with people. Being socially competent in the broadest sense is a twentieth century imperative. Of course, I mean far, far more than picking up the right fork, knowing when to wear gloves, and how to address a celebrity.

There are those psychological skills with economic results. Take the story of the lady shopping for a pair of shoes. She seated herself, and the young clerk removed her shoes. After measuring her feet, he simply said, "I find one foot is larger than the other." This remark offended her, and she stalked out of the store. Later in the day, as the story goes, she stepped into another shoe store. The salesman removed her shoes and measured her feet. He said, "Lady, I believe one foot is smaller than the other." She was elated and responded, "I thought that might be the case. The shoes are lovely. I'll take two pairs."

Then there are the tools of the professions and trades. Behind every competent medical doctor is a staff of capable teachers in medicine. Behind every competent attorney is a group of skilled teachers in law. Behind every competent tool made is a dedicated teacher or teachers. Behind every competent factory executive or supervisor are several devoted teachers. Behind every competent carpenter is, at least, one able teacher. Our list could easily and quickly become longer and longer.

Competence is certainly some of the power we associate with teaching. This is true whether it be in secular or religious education. Most of the time there is little need even to attempt to separate the two. Christian motivation should saturate all teaching. Let us look to another key word for assistance.

The teacher and his teachings are able to show us the need for *repentance*.

You and I are frail, weak, and sinful. We have all sinned by omitting and committing. Therefore, all are in need of asking for forgiveness. Who is in the best position to show us this? Isn't it the teacher? Even the preacher, as he reveals the need for repenting, is exercising the teaching prerogative of the ministry. Most of us have known teachers who, with a minimum amount of emotion, could make crystal clear the need for a human being to pray, "Oh God, I am truly sorry."

Leading one to see this need is always serious. However, there are many humorous stories relating to it. One is told of an errant Irishman named Patrick. It seems he had traveled across town during the night and stolen a basketful of fresh grapes from an outdoor market. They were a delectable delight, because Patrick dearly loved grapes. Within a few minutes, his conscience got the best of him. So he loaded them into his car and went to see Father Finnegan, to repent of his sin. He entered the confessional and said, "Your reverence, I confess that I stole a basket of luscious grapes." The priest replied, "Well, my son, you must do penance. You will have to swallow a dozen of them whole, one at a time." The worshipful silence was broken by Pat's uproarious laughter. Irritated, the priest asked for an explanation. Pat said in muffled sounds, "Wait until I tell my brother, Mike, who was with me. He stole four watermelons."

Two famous teachers help us to see. Thomas Carlyle said: "The greatest of all faults is to be conscious of none." Thomas Fuller said: "You cannot repent too soon, because you do not know how soon it may be too late."

The power to point out to us the need for repentance is unquestionably tied to good teaching. Again, this is true regardless of whether we are talking about secular or religious education. Sometimes we superficially divorce the two. Christian motivation should saturate all teaching. Another word asks to be heard.

The teacher and his teaching can cause us to acknowledge our *impotence*.

It takes the power of teaching to make our lack of power obvious to you and me. Effectiveness in any of life's pursuits is always tempered by our limitations. Our efficiency in the undertakings of this world can and often does break down, because of happenings over which we have little or no control. As we face the elements of the universe and one another, we are enfeebled by the simple fact of being human beings. Each of us is a little like the mentally deficient fellow who was proud of his physical prowess. According to his reasoning, he could leap over any stream—provided he could get a long enough running start. He came upon a stream that looked to be nearly ten feet across. He turned and walked a mile away from it, and then he began running toward it with all his might. Eventually arriving at the bank, puffing and huffing ferociously, he fell exhausted into the water head first.

The Apostle Paul was a great teacher who studied under Gamaliel. In II Corinthians, Paul asks to have his weakness taken from him. Then the master teacher taught him by saying, "My grace is sufficient for you, for my power is made perfect in weakness." Having admitted and accepted our Lord's truth, the Apostle could say, "for when I am weak, then I am strong."

This power to cause us to acknowledge our impotence is inspired teaching at its best. To be allowed a clear view of what we cannot do and do not know is a rightful expectation from great teaching. Be it secular or religious education, the same things hold true. Christian motivation should saturate all teaching. A final and, perhaps, most significant word demands a hearing.

The teacher and his teachings are able to reveal, before our eyes, God's *omnipotence*.

Try measuring the might of a Being unlimited by anything or anyone, except his own will. All power is His. Any power that we may have is delegated to us by Him. His power had no beginning and has no ending. Only good teaching can give us even an elementary understanding of what this means. You and I are a part of the Creation because God says so. Our very existence is utterly dependent on His omnipotent will. Bishop Reginald Heber was a brilliant clergyman in the Church of England. He has given to us a hymn that conveys this idea quite unlike any other. It appears in all major Protestant hymnals.

Holy, holy, holy! Lord God Almighty
All Thy works shall praise Thy name
in earth and sky and sea;
Holy, holy, holy! Merciful and Mighty
God in three persons, blessed Trinity!

The words tell us that His omnipotence allows for mercy. They further tell us that He is at work as Father, Son, and Holy Spirit.

In a wondrous way, such power, limited only by His own will, is a comforting thing. Do you know or have you ever known anyone with whom you would want to entrust this might? We are safe in His hands. To put our trust in any other is to ask for a pointless existence. Our optimism should abound! The Christian religion, at its core, is unwaveringly optimistic.

So the power of the teacher and his teachings enable us to perceive the almighty power of God. All education of lasting value does this. Christian motivation, especially at this point, should saturate all teaching.

Is it any wonder that the text from the Letter of James says what it does? To be a teacher is to have great responsibility. The power is so far-reaching, it is hard to measure with the most perfectly balanced scales or exacting yardstick. Those who teach are to be judged with "greater strictness."

Some of us are justifiably concerned about the standards of today's teachers—wherever, whoever, and whatever they are teaching. Are they giving us competence? Are they showing us the need for repentance? Are they causing us to acknowledge our impotence? Are they opening before our eyes the omnipotence of God? Such power is in their hands. If we believe the Holy Scriptures, they must give a strict accounting before their God.

PRECARIOUS PREDICAMENT

For where jealousy and selfish ambition exist, there will be disorder and every vile practice.

—*James 3:16*

Life itself is a precarious predicament.

You and I did not ask to come into this world. Had it been left up to us, some might have chosen otherwise. The ups and downs are sometimes like the ride on a roller coaster. There are days when it is quite a ride. There is boredom, too. Life is sometimes the greatest pain. One of the finest Christian spirits I ever met said, "Son, there are more downs than ups in this life." For her, I am certain this was true. At times, our Lord must have thought the same thing, and yet, His life, death, and resurrection were supreme victories. The pessimist can always moan, "I didn't ask for this life, which continually kicks me in the shins and then closes out with a few shovels of dirt to cover my remains." The Christian is an optimist, because he can't help being anything else.

Even though we did not ask to come into this world, we have been given strength to confront it. This should prevent us from becoming fatalistic and distressingly negative. Life is a gift. What we do with it is largely up to us.

We have all been in tight, explosive situations in this life. The Letter of James lends a personal and practical hand in identifying such a situation: "For where jealousy and selfish ambition exist, there will be disorder and every vile practice." Note, there isn't a wasted word. There is neither varnish nor veneer. He calls a spade a spade. The words have a way of crushing rationalizations that last a lifetime. These rationalizations even find expression beyond the grave, long after the human beings involved have gone to receive whatever reward is due them. The text is speaking of a situation which exists or has existed in every culture. No system, democratic or communistic, has functioned in its absence. The perpetual power struggles in Washington and the Kremlin illustrate it very well. The history books give us examples galore. The battlefields have been drenched with blood and gore. Think of the community or communities in which you live and work. In all of them, corruption and hatred tell their story. This predicament is perhaps the most precarious one in which we can find ourselves. Who can doubt the doctrine of original sin?

If you are like me, numerous questions enter your mind as you read the verse. There is neither the time nor the space to list all of them. We say "jealousy, selfish ambition, disorder, and vile practice" are wrong. But why? We are prone to reply with meager concentration, "It's obvious." Is it?

There is a violation of the law of God which intends all men to be brothers. That's the answer, isn't it? Why is it a violation? There are three excellent reasons. You will discover all of them in every precarious predicament our text speaks about.

The first reason is the *exaltation of oneself*.

No one else really matters. Family, friends, associates, and acquaintances are of little importance. Capital "I" emblazoned on every relationship is of consistent significance. Taking very good care of "Number One" is the stuff out of which life is made. Some are uncanny in the logic with which they apply this. Some make no bones about it. This is what they believe and set out to practice. There is a certain low grade of honesty here, but let us not dignify it by calling it worthy of imitation.

Inborn self-preservation is not nearly enough. Seeking the usual needs and conveniences of life offers no satisfaction. Not only must the "I" be cared for, it must be elevated to august heights. To ward off an enemy and go safely on one's way seems normal. Those filled with jealousy and selfish ambition are not satisfied. The enemy must be made to look bad and exposed as dangerous to others. A plentiful supply of good food, quality clothing, and well-built homes are fine; but they don't do much for the person pictured, except as they serve to build his image and ego.

A godlike status is sought. Who wants to be human? Deification of a perishable *Homo sapien* is an ominously treacherous pathway. The Man of Steel, Joseph Stalin, has been praised or damned, depending upon the brand of communism in power. This is true with anyone who sets out to be a god. Here we witness the terrible twisting of man's creation in God's image, which in reality is our only valid claim to fame. This was meant to be our crown of glory. It was never intended to curse our immortal souls beyond recognition.

The laws of morality are suppressed by egomania. The person afflicted becomes a monster. The monster becomes his own lawgiver. The lawgiver becomes a means to elevate himself. At this stage, mirrors are insufficient, because they only reflect what they are supposed to reflect. Criticism is either unwarranted or the raving of a misguided soul. There is only one ultimate: the self needs to remain at the top of the heap. Morals are seen in the context of "whatever elevates me must be right."

What can the Christian say to all of this? Only God truly exalts anyone. Jesus Christ, His Son, says, "I am the way, the truth, and the life." Will you join me as we survey another reason?

The second reason is the *infatuation with self-seeking influence.*

To dominate institutions and organizations is the continual objective. Some servants of society have been destroyed by those who valued influence above their productive existence. Some bulwarks of brotherhood have been mutilated by those whose chief concern was influence over their beneficial workings. Our institutions may be purely an outgrowth of cultural conditions, but they are needed. Our organizations may likewise be products of a given time, place, and persons, but they too are needed. No one has the right to destroy or mutilate by insanely putting his or her heavy fingerprints upon everything. Some individuals are so in love with their powers of control that they are incapable of understanding *agape,* or brotherly love.

To manipulate people is a must. Do individuals matter to those possessed by jealousy and selfish ambition? The answer is loud and clear. Yes—as instruments to channel one's abnormal attraction to influence strictly for personal gain.

The greatest good for the greatest number is a foreign idea. What may be good for the many gives way to the imprint of "number one." This is done by simply not permitting such an idea into one's frame of reference. If it is not there to receive consideration, it has no possibility of being implemented. The measurement of *a* good or *the* good is uncomplicated. One merely asks the question, What will keep my present influence intact and what can I do to extend it? Other influences are not weighed on their merits. They are given lip service. Concepts that could possibly erode one's overshadowing dominance are predetermined to have no merit. The news has to be managed, so that control will not slip away or diminish. Isn't it interesting how many police states exist or potentially exist in our own nation? "Freedom" may very well be our most misused term.

What can the Christian say to all of this? Only God can and does ultimately influence anyone or anything. Jesus Christ, His Son, says, "But woe to you, scribes, and Pharisees, Hypocrites! because you shut the kingdom of heaven against men; for you neither enter yourselves, nor allow those who would enter to go in." We might add: "The only difference between men and little boys is the price of their toys."

Won't you join me for a final reason why the precarious predicament in question is a violation of God's law?

The third reason is the *degradation of everyone else.*

35

No other person can speak with authority. Every deeply religious person knows with certainty and feels deeply that he or she is inspired from time to time. This gives none of us a corner on the market of inspiration. The personality saturated with jealousy and selfish ambition does not begin to develop at that point. Whether it be the authority of inspiration or some other, he or she is the only one capable of commanding and enforcing. The only technique every other person needs to know is how to obey. Subservience is an expected mode of acting and reacting.

People are pawns. God did not give us life to be subjected to someone's whims, but we are subject to "disorder and every vile practice." I cannot imagine anything much worse. We were created by God and for God.

Respect for human dignity and worth is invariably missing. No one who stands on his self-constructed platform and peers out across the multitudes can see their faces of joy and sorrow, and their just wanting to be somebody. Our Lord walked and talked among the people. To pontificate the message from His Father would have sealed its doom. Instead of ringing with vitality and the promise of eternal life, it would have been given a convenient burial among the works of other religious teachers and prophets. The personality held securely in the clutches of a precarious predicament may have little or no connection to racism. The color of skin is immaterial, as long as everyone stays in his or her secondary position.

The great men and women of the past are labeled usable or nonusable. A careful piece of editing goes on in the mental machinery. The very concept of greatness is ripped apart by those allocating inferior positions to others. The question asked in the dark, demonic recesses of one's soul is, "Will the words of highly respected, even idolized, figures leave me in the limelight?" It is a mania, isn't it? It isn't something we can conscientiously relegate to communism, is it? It is a fact of life wherever we find "jealousy and selfish ambition."

What can the Christian say to all of this? Only the

everlasting God measures value and values. Jesus Christ, His Son, says, "You shall love your neighbor as yourself."

By way of conclusion, we need to discern two all-important differences.

Let us recognize the distinction between jealousy and vigilant attitudes. To be critical of another's success is not necessarily jealousy. Success which runs rampant may be the result of scores of people getting hurt in their business and personal lives. As Christians, we are the watchdogs, so to speak, of society. At its deeper levels, the Christian spirit is always a reformation program in operation. People are not the way they should be—including ourselves—and God expects us to be sensitive to this. There is no indication in the Bible of our Lord ever being jealous of the worldly powerful scribes and pharisees. He did speak often about their religious establishment, which He usually characterized as hyprocrisy.

Let us also be quick to recognize the distinction between selfish ambition and healthy competition. It is doubtful if anything of consequence is ever accomplished without some degree of competition. Even though communism has damned the capitalistic competitive spirit, communists have found it indispensably useful! Psychologists tell us that we all need occasional personal victories in competition with others, just to have good mental health. Selfish ambition is eventually always vicious, malicious, and venomous. Recall the text says, "disorder and every vile practice." Yet, we are made to compete. That rugged competitor, the Apostle Paul, points out, "Do you not know that in a race all the runners compete, but only one receives the prize? So run that you may obtain it."

We must not violate God's law that all men are meant to be brothers. It has been pointed out why this particular precarious predicament is a violation of that law. Let us mistake neither jealousy for vigilance nor selfish ambition for wholesome competition.

THAT FIRST STEP

Draw near to God and he will draw near to you.
—*James 4:8*

How many times have we heard, "You take the first step"?
It would be very time-consuming to take an accurate count.
The reaction is so natural, we just expect it. It doesn't take any
unique brilliance to predict so-and-so will say, "Oh, you go
ahead." The routine of daily living is made up of this attitude.
Sometimes we feel others are just plain stubborn. Other times
we know they are timid. Still other times we see the legitimacy
of someone not wanting to be featured in the limelight.

People are usually hesitant to get their feet wet, regardless
of the circumstances. Maybe, as some philosophers say, man
is born a conservative. Maybe he is just anxious to see if the
other person will make a fool of himself. Maybe he is playing
it cool. For whatever reason, we know the truth involved. We
like the safety and security of well-worn patterns. Why
venture into the unknown, even if it appears to be a needed
journey?

What we have been saying in general terms is just as
true—if not more so—in the spiritual sense. The Christian
experience is a personal adventure with God. When it is trite
and meaningless, we have settled for less than an adventure.
Dynamic Christians are continually stepping out into the
unknown. We are creatures of creativity and innovation. Yet,
too often we are tagalongs. If other segments of society will
take the initiative, then we will be ready to try it as Christians
and as a church. Many have become so accustomed to the
church's attitude of hesitancy, they just expect us to come
along later and bless some technological or sociological

38

accomplishment. No one likes to be told by a pompous churchman or clergyman what he can or cannot do. On the other hand, let us not embarrass our faith and damn our churches by always saying, "Oh, you try it first." The churches across our land are sluggish giants wielding little power, spiritual or otherwise. The same applies to each of us as individual Christian church members. Who wants to take the first step in *genuinely* drawing near to his God?

James presents us with a gloriously promising command: "Draw near to God and he will draw near to you." Growing out of what has previously been said are two interrelated questions: Why don't we draw near to God? How can we destroy those things getting in our way? To deal with just one or the other leads to massive frustration. They belong together. So, let's communicate in terms of barriers and bulldozers.

What are the barriers that keep us from drawing near to God?

Fear. We are just afraid to take that first step. There seems to be lead in our feet. Someone will surely make fun of us. God will know us as we really are, and we are afraid of that. We are frightened by the possible pain if God discovers us as we are. As long as we stay out of range and "play religion," things don't appear to be too bad. Let us visualize ourselves coming into the presence of a perfect and holy God, here and now! This is fearsome business!

Self-righteousness. "I've already been baptized." "I've already taken the vows of the church." "Years ago I was received by the right hand of fellowship." "I haven't missed paying my pledge for forty years, and some of those were depression years." "I grew up in the church." We are well acquainted with the symptoms of this rather common ailment. From a strictly objective viewpoint, it is living with a lie. Our Lord's greatest barrier during His ministry was the self-righteousness of a privileged religious elite. They eliminated not only their possibilities of drawing near to God, but those of others as well.

39

Indifference. The most pronounced negative attitude every minister sees in our land in regard to Christ and His Church is "it doesn't make any difference." When one thinks and feels this way, drawing near to God is of little consequence. God doesn't count—except as the giver of all things. Those of an indifferent bent are not apt to admit God is the source of all things. "Maybe he is, maybe he isn't" is the reaction. "Jesus was born, lived, died, and some say arose from the dead. So what? The Church may be the Body of Christ and a fellowship of believers, but of what value is this to me?" Indifference to God is born of an infantile arrogance. It reminds one, upon occasion, of a baby blissfully enjoying his pacifier.

Greed. "The love of money is the root of all evil" has been quoted and misquoted for centuries. Of course, we often have to look much further than stacks of green bills to know anything about greed. For the greedy person, money may be supremely important, because it translates into power and recognition. Greed's twin sisters are control and domination. Greed looms large, as one perceives the need to approach God.

Sentimentality. The professional ministry has been maimed by "stained-glass pulpiteers" with syrupy clauses and phrases dropping harmlessly about the sanctuaries. The laity has been polluted with "pious Petes" who had all the right gospel words and could belch them forth upon a moment's notice. You and I may know the approved words, emote at the appointed times, and call upon God in a beautiful display of staged righteousness. What a barrier! Whole generations have been deprived of their religious usefulness. If we must, let us sound those pious trumpets; but if we be actors and actresses on a stage, then let us say so.

Legalism. Sometimes a good thing can be overdone. Certain disciplines of the mind and spirit may rob us of the spontaneity of the Holy Spirit. We cannot press this Spirit into a mold. We can and do allow it to work through our worship services and other times when we congregate together. It may

40

be time to say the same prayer you have said faithfully every morning for the last twenty years, but this may not be a means of drawing near to God. It may simply be a discharging of a religious duty, which has become empty and dulling to the spirit. The rigidity of performing worthy disciplines can immobilize us for practical, day-by-day living.

Hatred. When there is hatred in our hearts, we have a formidable barrier. It may be for a person or a group of persons. We do hate "in particular" and "in general." In either case, damage is being done to ourselves. It, perhaps like none of the others, is spiritually suicidal. It is a barrier with few if any equals.

Why don't we draw near to God? There are, at least, the seven reasons mentioned. All of them are well known in the depths of our souls—some better than others. Together or individually they are dreadful barriers. How can we bring them crashing to the ground?

What are the bulldozers that are able to destroy those things which get in the way of our drawing near to God?

Honesty. We are all a little like the fellow who says how much more effective he is after a twenty-minute coffee break. After awhile, he begins to doubt the truth of the time element. Yet, he keeps telling himself how wonderful he feels after that twenty minutes. Then after a period of weeks, his employer hands him a sheet for the previous week with precise times on it. Monday he took thirty-one minutes, Tuesday twenty-nine, Wednesday thirty-five, Thursday thirty-six, and Friday thirty-four. Exaggeration is a common failing, and fishermen are not the only culprits. When it comes to approaching our God, honesty is always the best policy. It bulldozes away some of the most strange and cherished objects.

Courage. After all the relevant words have been spoken, courage must be enacted to take that first step. The interesting thing about it is that no one can bottle it up and dispense it at will. Even the most powerful of churches cannot do that. The timid person can have a courageous spirit. The

41

modest person is not left deficient. After all, we are speaking of something which does not demand any form of fanfare. Courage is that imperative bulldozer. To draw near to God is another way of saying courage is already present.

Faith. Mountains of glib words are said about faith in a myriad of ways. In a religious sense, only the Apostle Paul's definition stands the test of time. He says, "Now faith is the assurance of things hoped for, the conviction of things not seen." The hard-nosed skeptic may respond, "Ah, yes, believing what you can't prove." To which you and I may reply, "But that is so inadequate." It is that, to be sure, but it is damagingly more. The skeptic's way is an attempt at clever simplicity, which tempts the unwary and occasional Christian pilgrim. Faith is a destroyer, in that it pushes aside the damnable debris between us and God.

Reverence. Many of our youth on the college campuses have been labeled unpatriotic. Are they also irreverent? I am afraid the answer has to be yes in some cases. But what about those in their thirties, forties, fifties, and older? There is not as big a generation gap in the religious sphere as we sometimes would like to think. Perhaps those of us over thirty are merely generating a gap to take the pressure off our own sins of irreverence, exemplified by our own lack of commitment to Christ and His Church.

Love. Through the ages, the poets have nearly sung humanity to sleep with love, by dramatizing and philosophizing. The theologians have tried to explain it by categorizing and systematizing. Can we afford to make it too difficult for our little minds? To know God is to love God. Love is mystical but practical, and only the life and death of Jesus Christ accurately illustrate it. The "love chapter" in I Corinthians labors in glorious language to define it. Upon reading the chapter again and again, I am still left with the impression that the Apostle Paul only humbly marvels at it. Praise God, love does obliterate that which seems immovable!

Humility. "The obvious never gets done" may be a cliche,

but the truth imparted is sometimes earthshaking. Do we know we must be humble to draw near to God? Do we hear "oh, you go first" reverberating in the background? How easy and natural it is for us to talk about someone else not being humble! Let us not mistake it for spinelessness. Witness the obedience to humility of our Lord during those very last days of His life. All barriers—even death—were conquered. *Trust.* Fully trust Him just once—the devils will run for cover. Our coins are imprinted with the motto In God We Trust. Shouldn't the Christian churchmember be able to say even more? Have you ever prayed "oh God, I am totally Yours"? Such a prayer is awesome and a heaven-sent bulldozer.

How can we destroy those things which get in the way of our drawing near to God? There are, at least, the seven divine tools mentioned. Thank God, some Christian churchmembers know and utilize them in superbly priceless ways. Together or individually they are miraculously effective bulldozers.

Let our remarks not degenerate into a subtle self-salvation. Let us utilize the intelligence and emotion God has given to us. His promises are gloriously true! Draw near to God. Then, He will draw near to you.

DECISIVE DEFINITION

Whoever knows what is right to do and fails to do it, for him it is sin.

—*James 4:17*

A somewhat calloused father of three teenagers went to his church's worship service. It had been several weeks since he worshipped God in a congregational setting. He was inspired by each part of the service. The offering was taken, and he made up his pledge. Then the pastor began preaching. It was a well-planned and delivered sermon. The father couldn't say that he was necessarily moved, either intellectually or emotionally. Finally the benediction was pronounced, and soon afterward, he arrived at home. The mother, who normally went to the service, asked him about the sermon. He replied, "Well, the pastor talked about sin." She answered, "Did it help you to understand yourself and family any better?" He replied, "I'm not sure." Pressing a little further, she inquired, "Well, what did he say about sin?" Quickly and with a wry smile he said, "Oh, he's against it like he's supposed to be." Such, I fear, is the fate of many sermons on this topic. It may be the unwillingness of the lay person to listen. It may be the preacher's lack of realism when encountering the Holy Scriptures.

Being spiritually realistic about sin is neither negative nor unconstructive. It seems we have made a fetish of what to do and what not to do, so that we can somehow qualify as sinning or not sinning. Of course, if this is carried to the nth degree, we are about where the scribes and pharisees were in our Lord's Day. We are in a humanly impossible situation. We can be in straitjackets that keep us from any kind of creative

44

tension with the world. If there is anything you and I should be learning, it is that the old passes away and the new must emerge. More than a few essentials of the Christian faith are hard to come by. The Letter of James gives us a "diamond in the rough" concerning sin.

Is it realistically possible to define sin? In James 4:17 we read: "Whoever knows what is right to do and fails to do it, for him it is sin." He dares to give us a decisive definition. There is nothing transitory about this. It is as practical and far-reaching an admonition as the human mind has ever encountered. As we polish this truth, certain essentially constructive elements in this definition begin to sparkle. What are they?

In the first place, the definition is *personal and subjective*. Each separate and distinct individual is asked to admit, "I am responsible." Before Almighty God, no one can take your place and no one can take mine. A saintly mother cannot do it. A godly father cannot do it. No religious genius can do it. The weight of such words in a society which tends to shift responsibility from a person to persons or to an organization is sometimes frightening. Of course, we are responsible, whether or not we acknowledge it. Knowing what is right and doing it cannot seriously be delegated to someone else. A human being may be adroit enough to dodge the arrow marked "personal moral responsibility" for a time. No one can do this indefinitely. If you and I could permanently evade this awful thing, wouldn't it make life so much more pleasant? Wouldn't it be wonderful to wake up some morning and not be met by the sense of a deeply personal accountability? Jesus Christ suffered and died for each of us, and that makes you and me all the more personally liable for what is right. His coming to humanity gives an even heavier cross to individuals. At the same time, the attainable crown is completely free from all corrosion.

It is sometimes humbling to recognize that one is limited by who and what one is. You and I are taught this by our occupations and professions. Each of us, as parents and teachers, must communicate this in a moral sense to our children. Saint Paul says, "I do the very thing I hate." Religiously speaking, there is probably no better biblical illustration than this. Each of us is bound and entwined by his or her own subjectivity. A delightful and conscientious person said to me only the other day, "I feel so good to know I am reaching out of my own thoughts and feelings to help others, and then I discover this is simply a case of extending my own personal needs into the lives of others." So what is "outgoing" and "objective" in general appearance remains a happening for the person, within his own limitations. You and I are selfish even when you and I seem selfless. Let us not be critical and negative. God made us this way. Your moral perceptions come through your pipelines into your reservoirs. The same is true with me. How can it be any other way? Why should it be any other way?

When the pressures of this life become more burdensome, you and I would like to pick an argument with the text. "It's too bad the author doesn't know we live in a different age. He would have written differently today." Isn't that about our reaction? Few of us wear the cloak of responsibility without time-consuming rationalizations. You and I do like the appealing fulfillment of personal religion. It offers relevancy when nothing else can. Only the shallow thinker can speak of someone not being basically subjective. You and I have to be who and what we are. When you attempt otherwise, it is self-defeating. The same is true with me. So the text takes into consideration a very elementary truth about each of God's children. This is the first reason for it being a decisive definition.

In the second place, the definition is *impersonal and objective* in nature.

As we sin, lives that we know nothing about are touched. In this case, it is hard to improve upon the illustration of dropping a rock into a body of water and watching the circles ever widen. Certainly, as our world grows more and more populated, the opportunities for hurting others of the human race have been astronomically increased. We may never know or even suspect the injuries caused by our sins. Likewise, we can be victimized by those we have never seen and probably never will. Metropolitan areas of hundreds of thousands of people create innumerable chances for the impersonal infliction of moral damage. If every person is precious in the sight of God, then regardless of whom is affected by our sins, we must understand our actions to be sinful. It is the nature of sin to hurt those we do not and never will know. We can wreak havoc around the globe and beyond. "Am I my brother's keeper?" is that ancient but most up-to-date universal question. If *all* men are meant to be brothers, those millions now living who we can never know are, nevertheless, important to us. No one can live for very long in a constant state of anxiety concerning what his sins can do to unknown others. Everyone must be aware that every sin has the potential of far-reaching disaster in unprepared lives.

We have to be content to let the chips fall where they will. In this respect, we are called on to be objective. There is no other avenue open to us. In areas of conduct where there is doubt as to what is right, we are not bound to weep for those in the way at the wrong time. The same is true when we know we are right. The chronic worrier is often the one who is extremely frustrated by his inability to control the consequences of his action or inaction. We are not perfect! How often must you and I remind ourselves? We can and do hurt people. The mature Christian repents as an unknowing sinner and trusts the bad effects will be minimal. If we were to weigh morally every action and lack of action as to its outcome, we would hardly draw a breath. God understands this, and so must we. Perhaps in the next world things will be different. For now we are given this life to live.

Can we argue with the Letter of James in terms of its implied objectivity and impersonal implications? We can, and we usually manage to do this in some of our more intensely searching moments. This may be a sincere attempt on our part to say, "It isn't so. If we are Christians, we can avoid sinning against all people." Then, as you ponder this reaction, a Christian comes to mind who you thought sinned against you. You recall that he sincerely told you he was sorry, but that he really did not know why you were upset. He had done what he felt was right. Then you are left with that most uncomfortable thorn: "I have sinned, because of my bad feelings toward him." That isn't all. Unbeknown to you, he thinks over the situation, becomes angry, and swears energetically at a traffic officer he has never seen before. Some of our sins affect those we know and others we don't know, and there is very little we can do about it. So James considers another very elementary truth about all of us. This is the second reason for it being a decisive definition.

Let us look one more time to another positive element in defining sin, which carries even more authority than the initial two.

In the third place the decisive definition is *inclusive and conclusive.*

Our emphasis is on those things we omit. My, isn't it surprising how modern our message is! Our churches are not crippled by horrendous sins the members have committed. They are limping along because of those important things the members leave undone. Who do you know in your church who should be branded a wicked sinner? It is the continual omission of what is right that gives pastors ulcers and sleepless nights. James includes everything that we know is right to do, but refuse to do. Please note the word "refuse." Isn't this the most common reason the right actions do not get done? For those who placed primary emphasis on the Ten Commandments, which told them what not to do, James's words must have been hard to swallow. More pointedly, he was saying, "Include in your definition of sin those right actions you know are right, but do not do."

From a different viewpoint, we see those sins we commit are also covered. So, as we are about to say his definition is only partial and temporary we see this is not the case at all. He shuts the door on such thinking by concluding any argument that may still exist in our minds. What you and I would like to keep open-ended and improve upon suddenly shows itself to be what it is: a decisive definition of sin. The sins of commission are more evident to us. In fact, this is so much the case, we may poke fun at them when humor is not apropos at all.

So the text includes both the obvious and not so obvious sins and concludes by banishing any doubts as to its scriptural authority to speak with finality. Who can improve upon it? Why is there any need to?

If right and wrong are to have meaning, we must deal with this definition. It is so final, it makes us shudder. It is so relevant—even at this precise moment—that it gives our senses a fine cutting edge.

What are the practical, summary ideas? No one else but you can know what is right for you. Be satisfied with who and what you are. You will unknowingly hurt others by your sins. You are called upon to live every day knowing you cannot manage the consequences of your sins. Sins of omission are the most dangerous because of their subtlety. Sins of commission can sometimes be made to appear unimportant because we are prone to write them off as commonplace.

If sin is a fact of life, try defining it without the fourth chapter and seventeenth verse of the Epistle of James.

KEEPING YOUR PROMISE

But above all, my brethren, do not swear, either by heaven or by earth or with any other oath, but let your yes be yes and your no be no, that you may not fall under condemnation.

—James 5:12

"Swearing" generally has two connotations in our society. One is negative: An argument arises. God's name is taken in vain. The air begins to turn the figurative blue with hot insults. Perhaps the only constructive thing to come out of such countless situations is that some people say they feel better. They say this stream of steamy profanity makes them more relaxed. In this sense, maybe they do have a point, but it is a weak one.

We consider the other connotation positive: A courtroom is well packed. The rightful verdict is dependent on the witness telling the truth. He enters a booth beside the judge. We hear the words, "Do you promise to tell the truth, the whole truth, and nothing but the truth, so help you God?" Then we hear an affirmative answer. It gives the situation an aura of divine respect, because we have heard of the penalties for perjury.

In our Lord's day swearing had to do with one's promise. It was a common practice to seal one's promise with an oath. It was a daily ritual for some. Some had developed it to a fine art. An uninformed and idealistic person could be greatly injured in a number of ways by not knowing the name of the game. You see, some oaths were all show and meant nothing in terms of keeping a promise. The intent to seal one's promise had been perverted into quite another thing. It made a travesty of truth.

The Letter of James calls our attention to a practical solution. We are given guidance by two "dos" and "don'ts." *Do make your promise without enforcing it with an oath.* Shouldn't this be expected of the Christian? The Christian brings integrity into every human relationship. The way he thinks and acts is an indicator. Sometimes those gauges and dials are too narrowly defined—we get the major and minor matters muddled. Even this state of affairs becomes productive, because the Christian spirit is the highest moral principle known to man. We may disagree vehemently, but everyone can still see the Cross of Christ with utmost clarity— and that is what counts.

Why should any Christian make a "big deal" about keeping a promise? Isn't that what is expected of us? Our Lord died that you and I might have our word taken in good faith. He did not merely tell others what truth was. He went about being the truth. Recall His words, "I am the truth. . . . " Indeed, aren't we speaking of a legitimate expectation from His followers? Think how much less morally complicated our world could be! Oh, if everyone's word were good, we would still need many, many written documents. We forget what we promise. Sometimes none of us has the capacity to remember everything promised. Yet, think of what it would mean just to know a person's simple promise was good! In our highly mechanized world, the very thought is comforting.

"Liar" carried very serious charges in the days of our fathers and grandfathers. In those days, a man's word was either good or it wasn't. "Let your yes be yes and your no be no" was understood as more than just a bit of romanticizing. I am not suggesting that if they were living in our day, present morality would be on a significantly higher plane. I do believe we needlessly talk ourselves into moral dilemmas. If making promises without swearing, either verbally or in writing, that they are true is old-fashioned and unrealistic, then I confess to being both. We can and do become entangled and befuddled in elementary moral relationships, because we are conditioned to do so. After all, if it is in vogue to make a simple promise as complex as possible, isn't that what we do?

So much for the first "do." The second one is easily overlooked.

Do be clear about any promise you make.

Some are long-term. That is, we make them with the full intention that they will be lasting. Perhaps the best example of all is the wedding vows. "Wilt thou love her, comfort her, honor and keep her in sickness and health; and forsaking all others keep thee only unto her so long as ye both shall live?" Then change the "her" to "him" and place the obligation on the other part of the marriage. In premarital counseling, one of the first questions I ask a young couple, each of whom have never been married, is, "Will you look forward to celebrating your golden wedding anniversary together?" If one or both are divorced, I ask, "Is this going to be the last marriage for both of you?" It is almost uncanny how surprisingly similar the reactions are. At first there is a smile and then a deadly serious stare at me or something in the study. A great deal of precious pastoral time is saved by these questions. In all areas of life, many promises are made which seem not to entail any commitment by certain parties involved. From the outset, it is known that the promises were never meant to be kept. It behooves each of us, first of all, to be honest with ourselves. Then we are not apt to drag others into relationships which leave their expectations unfulfilled.

Some promises are short term. A good example is one's financial pledge to his church. Generally, churches make this very plain by printing the time period on the commitment cards. It is just good Christian business to do it that way. If more than a year is involved, capable lay and clerical leaders will say so. Of course, the local church is a convenant relationship, with members depending on one another. Let's say a person agrees to take a Sunday school class for the short term of six months. He should not be teaching for six years without relief under the subtle duress of not being able to find a replacement. If it is short term, let it be understood that way. If it is indefinite, then let that be understood. If short term promises cannot be kept in the church, where can they be kept?

Thus, we have the two "dos" suggested by James. The two "don'ts" are equally important to our spiritual health. Let's take a look at them.

Do not play the part of a hypocrite, by promising something you do not intend to fulfill.

This is often done under pressure from another person or persons. It can be a knotty and explosive situation. Almost any kind of promise can be extracted from any individual at the proper pressure point. The moral weight of the whole matter then shifts back, at least to some degree, to the one turning the crank on the vise. Moral complexity and unnecessary bitterness are often the outcome. Having experienced such quandaries, you and I must recognize that adults are supposed to have a reasonable amount of maturity. To make a promise we know we cannot keep is immature action. It does not mean we can always know what ones we will be able to keep. It does mean we are not to be beguiled by what we know to be our weakness. Our Lord calls upon us not only to know more about ourselves, but to utilize what we already know. Not a single one of us knows exactly what he or she would do under some conditions. Yet, everyone of us who professes the name of Jesus Christ knows something about the presence of the Holy Spirit as counselor and guide.

Possession may be nine-tenths of the law, but intent is nine-tenths of morality. At first this may sound like the phrase "sincerely wrong." We have our good intentions, but they never seem to accomplish anything. Intent applies to the depths of our souls, where moral and religious decisions are made. Without a will of our own, of course, we are simply talking about animal instincts. Thanks be to our God, each of us has a will of his own! We are human beings created with moral responsibility and religious capacity. Joseph Stalin's daughter tells us her ruthless father deliberately set out to murder hundreds of thousands of his countrymen who opposed him. Measure this by the compassion of General Eisenhower, whose only purpose was to defeat a Nazi Germany determined to conquer the world. To be sure, both kept their promises, but my what a difference in intent! Some astute historian might remark, "Stalin was not hypocritical. He fulfilled his promise, and for him, it was a worthy one." As Christians, we should be quick to reply, "But if God cared so much for us that He allowed His Son to be crucified, how can we justify, in any way, the continued crucifixions of humanity by an atheistic and communistic philosophy unwilling to bend to Christian morality?

So much for the first "don't." The second refers to "applied vindictiveness."

Do not utilize an oath as an evil method to promise retaliation.

We all know the pattern. Joe Doakes does something that has the appearance of a personal affront. Whether it is deliberate or not, we cannot quite tell. We think it is. He doesn't make any attempt at restoration. He doesn't even bother to stick an olive branch into his Sunday suit coat. Well, justice has to be done. An ego with deepening abrasions just can't go unattended. There aren't enough bandages and jars of salve to treat all the injured places. So, we can't do something in a small way. Scripturally, we begin repeating "an eye for an eye and a tooth for a tooth" under our breath. Then we do it! Before God, we swear to get even. "If it's the last thing I ever do, I'll get him back—so help me God." That seems a little too mild, so we fortify it. "I'll right that wrong—in God's name." Can't we hear our Lord saying, "and a little child shall lead them." Children are angry as can be one day, and all is forgotten the next. They must find it hard to understand our grown-up oaths. Perhaps there is nothing, in the long run, more disillusioning to the wounded parties. We know of individual, one-to-one relationships that are tragic, family squabbles that are disastrous, national and international arguments that are incomprehensibly painful. The fact is, we are simply seeing the depths of our own sinful nature. The person carrying the loaded reprisal becomes disillusioned with himself for the limits to which he is willing to go. The person who sees the arsenal with his name on it becomes disillusioned by the magnitude of human depravity and its deliberate attempts at vengeance. Such is the case when, by swearing in the name of God, we nail the lid shut on the box filled with our hurt and the planned hurt of others. The box is a sealed coffin containing malice which should be buried, but is not. It is grotesquely carried from one place to another.

So we have spoken about the two "don'ts" given expression by James.

There are days when we seem to be living in moral jungles. Only occasionally can we make out a shaft of light through the closely placed trees and dense underbrush. Aren't all promises made to be broken whenever we decide the conditions are right? Let us pray for a rescue party to lead us out of the presence of monkeys jabbering double-talk and snakes hissing the cleverness of expediency.

Why does James warn us about sealing our promises with oaths? For the same reason that our Lord spoke to His Jewish brethren about an essentially high moral and religious plane. His disciples have no need to seal their promises. They don't promise things they do not intend to fulfill. They are clear about the promises they make. They have no need to promise retaliation—even with an oath.

RATING OUR PRAYERS

The prayer of a righteous man has great power in its effects.

—*James 5:16*

Prayers do not have the same value. Both intuition and experience tell us this is the case. We know of those who seem to open the very windows of heaven. We know others who cannot keep from repeating dead phrases that just will not come to life. It is true around the world. Some prayers have what it takes. Others do not. Still others are in that vast mediocre land where there is enough life to make us listen, but enough death to put the brakes on inspiration trying to be born. How would you rate yours? Have you stopped to look at them with care recently? Do you mean what you say? Do you say what you mean? Prayers are the stuff out of which life is made. I don't believe there is any man or woman who has never prayed. You and I can't keep from it. Having admitted this, we still recognize a big, big difference in our prayers. Some of us sincerely wish all of them would spring forth from our hearts and minds crystal clear and power filled.

The Letter of James tells us of one kind of prayer that is powerful: "The prayer of a righteous man has great power in its effects." From this we could launch into many hundreds of words about what it means to be righteous. We might dwell upon the magnificent prayers made by men and women in close communion to their God. It would be worthwhile to point out at length how necessary it is to become a strong Christian before our prayers can have power in them. Surely you can think of other roads on which our text is able to take us. Let us move in what may be a totally new direction for some. Will you unite with me in thought and emotion while we perform a much needed analysis?

To rate our prayers, it seems to me that we must first divide them into two categories: There are the basically constructive and helpful ones; there are the basically destructive and hurtful ones. There are five kinds in each category. Each of them lends itself to an easily remembered word, and the words easily relate to one another.

Let us take a look at those classified *constructive and helpful.*

The first prayer *refuses* obstructions. It is a disciplined prayer. Nothing is allowed to enter into this relationship with God which might destroy its impact. It calls upon God in complete openness. It forsakes one's own little worlds. It enters into a new perspective, calling for help and guidance on His terms. Pipelines previously robbed of their usefulness by grime and dirt were cleared by a disciplined detergency with imperative assistance from the Divine. The healing waters of the Holy Spirit are then able to flow to a thirsty soul. It is a prayer that in time and in fact is a conversation with our Creator. It does not presume man's worthiness to talk with God as an equal. It does start out with the truth of His caring deeply for man, in spite of man's own unworthiness. A major key to prayer practiced by our Blessed Lord was to refuse persistently those things that might block communication with His Father.

The second prayer *peruses* someone else's prayer. The Lord's Prayer is our classic example. It can only be meaningful *if* we pay close attention to the words while we are saying them. Just to mouth the clauses and phrases of this prayer of all prayers is a spiritual depressant. In a way, two activities should be going on at the same moment. One is the repeating of the words, and the other is the process of coming to terms with what they are saying to us. In a sense, all prayer is like this. However, it is another's prayer which must receive this treatment for it to be a worship experience. Think how many

57

times we pray another's prayers! Our devotional booklets, hymnals, and Bibles all contain some real jewels; and we utilize them. The words, to be meaningful, must become ours, and to do this, the time has to be taken to peruse or look closely at them.

The third prayer *amuses* ourselves and others. Humor is good for any spiritual pilgrim. Something funny will open doors that nothing else seems capable of opening. Prayer can be just a long-faced exercise in piety. Part of our problem is that we only go to God when we are in trouble or think we are. I suppose none of us can picture God joking and having a good time. Didn't Jesus? Look into the Gospels of Matthew, Mark, and Luke. One biblical scholar tells us forty-four laughter-provoking sayings of Jesus are recorded. It is possible to be serious and humorous at the same time. In your prayers before you retire this night, talk to God about the ludicrous things you and others have done. Learn to laugh about them. God will hear every word you say. Amusing prayers are excellent therapy for the souls that are uptight.

The fourth prayer *transfuses* another with a needed quality. Our Lord leads us in pathways that enable us to do many wonderful things for ourselves and others. From time to time, we are shown, as the dawning of a cloudless summer day, a quality someone needs. Maybe it's respect, persistence, bravery—or something else. In any event, our Lord shows us what is required and expects us to do our part by praying that the person will receive a gift He has ready in waiting. Spiritual freedom is one of the great blessings of the Christian faith. Have you been shown that a friend needs to be more kind toward himself and others? Ask God that he might have kindness. This type of prayer works untold miracles that we take for granted. I venture to say that all of us have been helped at least once by a power-packed transfusion through prayer.

The fifth prayer *diffuses* inspiration. Everyone is capable of making this prayer. It is one that works like a shotgun blast.

The pellets are spread over a wide area. It thrills the heart and makes the mind razor sharp. It is as if the voice of God were speaking. Of course, He does speak through our prayers. It is for Him to know the time, place, and person. Who among us can say with any responsibility, "I shall now speak for God"? Yet, we are able to diffuse innumerable drops of divine influence with His guiding hand.

I would be the first to admit these five constructive and helpful prayers are not all-inclusive. Perhaps you have already thought of a sixth or seventh one. In any event, let us freely acknowledge those cited and give them a premium rating.

Let us apply our critical faculties as we examine another five categories of prayer classified *destructive and hurtful.*

The first prayer *excuses* ourselves. It is one of those prayers that slips out so gracefully. "Oh Lord, I didn't aim to, but I did." "Dear God in Heaven, that was wrong, but I couldn't help it." "Our Father, I knew that was the right thing to do, but I just didn't do it." This type of prayer seldom does anything beyond saying, "Excuse me." It is a watered-down attempt at repentance. It may appear mannerly and in good taste to us, but we are not talking to someone who is primarily concerned with social amenities. We are praying to the living God!

The second prayer *abuses* the Holy Spirit. This prayer is the worst of all. In the words of Saint Paul, it "grieves the Spirit." It goes contrary to the guidance and counsel of God. We have all been guilty. We are inspired to lift up a certain person in prayer. We dispel the thought. We are inspired to ask for strength for our church. We dispel the thought. We are inspired to confess a sin. We dispel the thought. The list seems to go on *ad infinitum.* This prayer throttles essential workings of the spirit. It acts as an instrument of spiritual suffocation. Too often we carelessly forget that the third part of the Trinity is the Holy Spirit. It is a very real force, with a mystical and yet rational personality all its own. May you and I not abuse it!

The third prayer *accuses* a brother and begins, "O God,

now I know he did that, it's wrong, and it seems to me it's time for punishment." Like so many other things in our lives, this, too, boils below the psychological surface and then oozes into our prayers almost unnoticed. Then it can dominate them. Accusations wear many faces. They can become entire prayers. With our world aflame, surely we as Christian members of the Church can do better. Our faith and the Body of Christ are given to be the saving factors in a degenerating and dying world. We cannot afford to clutter our prayer lives with such wanton waste. As you enter your private rooms for prayer, pause to recognize any temptation you may have to make your words a tragic exercise in accusing fellow pilgrims.

The fourth *confuses* ourselves and others. Do you take a clear mind into your prayer sessions? Oh, it is comforting to know our Lord hears our incoherent desperation. As we pray alone, do we know what to say? Perhaps our mental jumblings and emotional mix-ups are carefully understood by our Heavenly Father. Do we understand them? You and I need to state audibly or inaudibly whatever prayer we offer. This is not for God. It is for our own good. When another hears us and can only decipher broken threads of meaning, we add their frustrations to our own. If you are having trouble with prayer words and ideas, sit down and write out what you mean. Then rewrite what you really want to say. Confusion has a way of lifting almost miraculously at the close of the rewriting. It is ego satisfying and spiritually uplifting to pray again and again a prayer you have written. Share it with your friends and families. Some of our bewilderments during times of prayer are so unnecessary.

The fifth prayer *misuses* confidences. It is an easy one to make because we repeatedly pray before we think. There are few things in life more precious than confidences well kept. Confidential information that can hurt one or many must be jealously guarded. This prayer spells disaster in human relationships more definitely than the others mentioned. The gossip mills are always turning, and some grist is considered choice. To be of help to many persons means sealed lips, except in the privacy of one's own secret sanctuary. Lay and clerical counseling can be effectively done on no other basis. In short, pray for the one who has disclosed privileged information; but on your honor, hold it close to your heart.

Can you think of other destructive and hurtful prayers? Those just mentioned certainly deserve the rating of "very poor, unnecessarily costly, and unchristian." Therefore, you and I are summoned to stay away from them.

How about your prayers? Into which one of the two categories do most of yours fall? It is rather easy to fasten some of them on the preceding pegs, isn't it? So much of what you and I are is directly connected to our prayers—spoken and unspoken. Sometimes we can get lost in breaking down important experiences and analyzing them, because it can be a time-consuming effort. If we didn't seriously and conscientiously do this with prayer once in a while, our ruts would be so deep there would be no seeing out of them.

Will you promise yourself to do better? It is one thing to see a need in one's prayer life, and something else to do anything about it. Having seen at least some areas where improvement can be made, are you willing to act? It's an elementary question, and the spiritual life gets hung up more often here than at any other place. Let us pray for the strength to conquer those crucial moments and to use them to upgrade our prayers.